UNLEASHED

Discovering Your True Potential

BY

Rosze Kaur

About the Author

Rosze Kaur is an anointed teacher of God's Word. She was born and raised in Punjab, India in a small village called Awana. In 2001, she came to the United States of America in search of a better life. God has transformed the life of Rosze Kaur from Sikhism to Christianity. Rosze has dedicated her life to serving God and humanity. With unwavering compassion and faithfulness, it is her desire to help build a hope into God's people that will help them to live a life of victory! Rosze Kaur's passion is to see other people win in life.

TABLE OF CONTENTS

INTRODUCTION

This book starts with a promise. Read it and answer the questions thoughtfully, and you will live a better life. This book is titled **"Unleashed" Discover your True Potential** and that is really what happens when you read it, and thoughtfully answer the questions. Realize that reading this book alone is not enough, and that you must form new beliefs, new habits and spend the time necessary to learn more about who you are, what you are really good at, and how to put it all into practice. By following the steps outlined in this book, you will begin moving your life and career in the direction of your goal. You will also attain greater happiness, job fulfillment, financial rewards and a greater sense of self-worth and personal satisfaction than you ever thought possible. Got a pen? Good, then let's get started.

You have been asked a very simple question since you were barely able to speak - "Who are you?" You have likely answered it a hundred different ways, and your answer has probably changed significantly since you first answered it. The truth for most people is that you probably don't have any idea of who you really are. Think about it. You could answer this question in so many ways, using words like Father, Dancer, Sister, etc. You might also begin to think of yourself in adjectives, like gifted, curious, caring, etc. What matters most, is not only the time you spend on self-reflection, but also in seeing yourself through the eyes of others. Self-awareness is a tricky thing, often elusive. In fact, for some people the more you seek it, the harder it is to find. You may even feel at times like you are running in circles, and then suddenly something happens, and you have a revelation or an insight. Maybe at times like this you sit down and journal, or you share your new insights with others. You might even be prompted to write down some goals in light of new thoughts and feelings that you are having. Maybe you have never even written down your goals and aspirations - not a problem. Using this book, you will begin to discover what your God given talents are, how to translate your talents into goals, and how to engage a time-tested success formula that dates back thousands of years in order to define and live the life that you are most suited for; the life you have always wanted. This will enable you to give back to the world more than you ever thought you could before.

CHAPTER 1

Understanding Self Discovery

By virtue of the society we find ourselves in, self-discovery has become overrated. This may be because people are becoming more individualistic or because we tend to believe that we are not performing beyond "expectation". Most of the time, I hear people say *"I can't find my purpose"* or I just hear them lament *"I haven't discovered who I am"*

What exactly does it mean to discover oneself? Answer this question to the best of your understanding before going deeper in the book

____

____

____

____

____

____

So many believe self-discovery is a super-brain process which would 'boost' your lifestyle.

Many also believe that they are not living up to their full potential.

I wouldn't say these reasons are not justifiable or true, but I would like to say that most people don't really know what self-discovery means. Even those who have read books about this topic don't utilize the knowledge efficiently. So, the first thing we have to do here is understand what we really know to be self-discovery.

Answer below ''Why you are yet to discover yourself?''

____

____

____

Meaning Of Self-Discovery

Self-discovery according to Merriam Webster's Dictionary, it's the act or process of gaining knowledge of understanding of your abilities, character, and feelings. Self-discovery is a process that we must have experienced consciously or unconsciously at a time in our lives. This process affects the decisions we make, and it is eventually realized when it becomes possible for us to live peaceably with whatever those decisions may be. Self-discovery doesn't come because you are dissatisfied with your life as it is now; it doesn't come as a result of wanting to pursue happiness or achievement or goals. It doesn't only have to do with success or spiritual wisdom and knowledge like people say. Self-discovery is more than that. Self-discovery is about digging into your inner-self, to create a seemingly perfect world with which you are pleased to live in.

Factors That Helps In Self-Discovery.

Practical Life Experiences:

"Until you are faced with that situation, don't say you can handle it better." This statement is just the bitter truth. Until you are faced with a particular situation, you can never really predict how you would respond in it. When you think that you are going to act in a certain manner, you are just in the theory world which is far different from the practical world. Being open till the experience is actualized is the key to self-discovery in this instance. If there is a parallel realization between who we think we are and who we truly are in practice or reality, we are able to achieve that life that we can live peaceably with. We learn more about ourselves through experiences of life, and the accumulation of these experiences is what exposes us to understanding and learning more about who we are. All these come down to the fact that a fundamental requirement in this aspect for self-discovery which is of great benefit to us is to permit ourselves the freedom to lay open to new experiences when they uncover themselves. In contrast, when you hide from experiences as they present themselves, you hide from the real you, and this means that we do not want to find out the truth about ourselves. This behavior could stop you from having what you want, what is yours.

This doesn't mean that we should seek these experiences, but we should not hide from them when they present themselves.

List what you have discovered from yourself in the past through practical experiences.

____

____

____

____

____

____

____

Environment:

The environment we find ourselves in defines the person we are and the person we would become. Discovering who we are comes not only from the practical experience as explained above, but it also comes from what we have seen, what we see and what we wish to see. An element of the choices we make and the reasons for making such choices becomes a defining factor for self-discovery. If we become the type to make decisions based on what others think and not what we want, we have decided to choose that path. Contrariwise, if we realize that we are people who will stand up for our beliefs and principles despite the beliefs of others, or despite what others think or say, then that becomes another path we have decided to follow. The fact remains that the environment we find ourselves in or the environment we choose to build around us, makes us discover the type of person we are.

List what you have discovered from yourself while co existing in your environment.

____

____

____

____

____

____

Sacrifices:

A lesson in self-discovery which we cannot live without is sacrifice. It comes the point when we decide to go for something which is opposing to something else we have to make a personal choice. Well, this personal choice becomes one major element of self-discovery. Another element to sacrifice as a part of self-discovery is things or experiences we may have bypassed to make a personal decision. When we can live peaceably with this, then we have made an important discovery about who we are.

List all you have discovered from yourself in the past through being sacrificial.

____

____

____

____

____

____

____

____

Faith and beliefs:

We may hide from the fact that we are not "religious," but the truth is that we uphold a particular belief, and the defining moment of our life comes truly from our faith in the supernatural and our belief in people. We cannot afford to push away the fact that the elements of the spirit come and work with certain rules, and certain principles define the choices we make and the person we are. The Good book teaches humans to love the creator first and foremost; then it teaches us to love others (our neighbors) just as we love ourselves. Many more of these rules and regulations exist in the Good book which serves us physically and spiritually should we put our trust in the Creator. To some, true self-discovery comes only from the creator when we identify with the Good book.

Self-discovery works as a factor which enables us to live peaceably with any decision we make. We can understand ourselves perfectly through self-discovery whether it is reached through experience, responsibility, instinct or what we just feel comfortable with. The American English Dictionary defines self-discovery as: "becoming aware of one's true potential, character, motives, etc." Now, here comes the problem - can self-discovery only come by becoming aware of your true potential? We have established the fact that self-discovery means finding a purpose in life but one quick question: Do we all have a purpose? The answer to that could come from your instincts, but one thing is sure. We had a mandate to fulfill when we were welcomed to planet earth. A good process of self-discovery could begin when you start to dig deep into your childhood, and you set lose the experiences that shaped you, the good and bad. It has to do with understanding your beliefs and living by them no matter what. Self-discovery requires making some real tough decisions and sticking with them.

List out what you have discovered from yourself in the past through having faith and beliefs.

____

____

____

____

____

____

____

My concluding message about self-discovery here is that you should stop being your own worst enemy! Don't lie to yourself about your emotions and feelings; accept them and allow yourself to feel whatever you want to feel. The freedom is within you. The most important thing now is for you to know that the main aim of self-discovery is freedom. Love the universe, and the universe will give you back that love.

Below, list up to 10 things/events that you would like to experience in the near future. Make sure that these desires stem from the heart and soul and not from fear or ego-

based thinking. Also, don't limit yourself through your own beliefs about what you can have or do in this world.

MY DESIRES

1._______________________________________

2. ______________________________________

3._______________________________________

4._______________________________________

5._______________________________________

6._______________________________________

7._______________________________________

8._______________________________________

9._______________________________________

10._______________________________________

CHAPTER 2

The Essence of Self Discovery

"When I discover who I am, I'll be free."-Ralph Ellison, Invisible Man

This book may not perform the function it is supposed to, if we fail to know the essence of self-discovery and the purpose of discovering your potentials. The effects of self-discovery include happiness, fulfillment, clarity, and enlightenment. The journey of self-discovery is worth taking for the following reasons:

Self-discovery leads you in choosing the right career. The forces of self-discovery enable you to look inward to find your inborn talents. It is going to help you utilize your peculiar capabilities. Self-discovery makes you understand whether you are a generalist or specialist. You may be someone who focusses on quantity rather than quality or quality over quantity. You may be someone who is comfortable in rigid environment, or someone who needs more flexibility. It's nice to know that when you acknowledge your mental and physical strength, you are able to pursue a career which gives you joy, satisfaction and money. This is one of the benefits and reasons why self-discovery should be taken seriously.

Self-discovery improves relationships: It is no news that people find fulfillment in others. Self-discovery involves knowing who you truly are and establishing yourself with that one particular person. You don't need approval from anyone else before you become comfortable with the person you are or your true self. Self-discovery helps you to remove the wrong person from your life. It eliminates the critical, negative energies and puts you on the right path with individuals who will love you for who you are. It is not a crime to say that finding a spouse is self-discovery on its own because you can certainly discover yourself in the person you want to spend the rest of your life with.

Self-discovery makes us physically healthy: The WHO gave us a broad definition of health, this includes mental health. It is important to know that there is no question that self-discovery or self-awareness makes us mentally healthy, it can improve our physical health. This happens when you begin to value yourself more. The process of eating better, getting out, and giving your body what it truly wants comes from the fundamental thought that you are now satisfied with who you are and you enjoy who you are.

William Barclay says, "There are two great days in a person's life. The day we are born, and the day we discover why."

Just as there are benefits in self-discovery, the immense benefits of knowing your purpose cannot be over-emphasized. Indeed, it is becoming increasingly apparent day by day that knowing and understanding your life purpose is the most important step in individual development. Living on purpose sends the problems which you may face in life away from your window. Don't get me wrong; this doesn't mean that you will not face challenges, no! Problems will come, but they are stepping stones to break through. Ultimately, when you live a purposeful life you live at your best. Quickly, I would like to explain some benefits that follow those who search for their life purpose, and understand their life purpose and chase after it.

Focus: Knowing your life purpose makes your lifestyle become a truing mechanism. This doesn't mean you would live like a robot or a boring life, but you would be able to make core decisions, and the roadmap to your success is already at your fingertips. Knowing your life purpose channels your life, your time, your investments, your energy, your money, and talents into the right thing. It directs those things into what you enjoy, what you love doing, what you are born for. It makes living fun and success achievable. Sadly, the other side of the coin is that most times, a life of purpose is scattered and unfocused. It's like a boat having no rudder, but when your true purpose is discovered, your life can be shifted to a place where the currents of circumstance ebb.

Passion: For most people, the process of clarifying their life purpose unlocks the key to the passion of life. This passion becomes the gasoline to propel their life forward. This happens in extraordinary ways. While a life without purpose or off purpose is often bereft of any real passion, a life with purpose is full of passion. Have you ever wondered why some people keep changing jobs or have a lackadaisical attitude to the one they have now? It's very easy, passion. When passion exists, the experience of the individual becomes more like a "Pleasantville." I am sure you know the movie.

Fulfillment: A life of expression is fulfilled when you have discovered your purpose, and you are allowing it to guide or affect your decisions. As we have established earlier, a life of purpose is full of meaning, and people who have realized their purpose definitely make a difference in this world. People off purpose lead a meaningless life, and they attribute their qualities, beliefs, struggle and even grief to fear. Knowing your life purpose and discovering your full potential is a key to smacking fear out.

Being relentless: When an individual discovers his or her purpose, he/she becomes unstoppable. In the long run, an individual who has found his/her purpose finds a potential to total satisfaction in life. It is not obligatory for you to live your life like a bull, ramming through anything which finds its way to you. When you discover your purpose, patience, persistence and high power to succeed is made available for you. But people who are off the grid of success, find themselves stuck in life. This is not surprising because they have failed to tap into their passion, and they seem to be like a high-powered automobile having no fuel in the tank.

Integrity: A life on purpose is a life having ultimate and definitive integrity. A life full of integrity is a life that is whole and complete.

People of integrity are those who have established their purpose and are actually living it. Those who are full of integrity live to their core values as they serve themselves and others through the manifestation of their life purpose. Those who are living off purpose simply haven't discovered who they are; they haven't found who they are. Don't get me wrong, nothing is actually wrong with them, something is just missing, and that is purpose.

I want to use the latter part of this chapter to expose you to seven ways to self- discovery; seven ways to finding yourself in you. The next chapter is going to discuss the understanding of your full potential. Discovering the real you is a personal roadmap to what makes you the real you. Learning to tune out the harmful broadcasts is in your head could be the first step.

Use positive affirmations and some splendid attributes to trade any negative inner voice which may want to deter you from self-discovery.

Setting your sights high and your tune perfect are good attribute on the journey of self-discovery. Your destination and how you can achieve your goals can only be set by you and no one else. Then we have to come to a conclusion that it is all about you, yes you, the selfish you, the true you.

In number two, we mentioned setting your tune. A good way to do that is to listen carefully with a trained ear for words of appreciation, encouragement, and compliments. Doing this pushes the negativity aside. Undoubtedly, you must have affected someone's life in a good way, just your smile to someone could make their day. Remind yourself of the good thoughts and compliments while you reminisce about your day anytime.

Another way to self-discovery is having the innocent lifestyle; take your time to think of the smile of a child, the pure heart without any hint of the "isms." The heart of an average adult is made of baggage which we must have collected along the way on the journey of life.

These baggage's fall under the "maturity approach", but these things tend to color our perspective about other things. We should sometimes return to the innocent stage in our life. Before we can return, we need to have the heart of a child, the knowledge of an adult, and the experience of a grown-up.

Fighting off depression: this is a good process in the self-discovery plan. Depression should not get you down; you should not shy away into a corner and alienate yourself from others. Instead, you should speak out. Get up, move! Find people, make that connection. A simple "excuse me" could go a long way in getting depression off. Making friends and speaking to acquaintances is a good way to fight depression, and when depression is eliminated, self-discovery is achieved.

Still buttressing the point above, making an effort to initiate conversations is a very good way to begin our journey of self-discovery. Kindness from friends and strangers help to get us out of the horrible huff. In fact, they make our day and eliminate depression thereby catapulting us to the world of self-discovery.

Treating negative situations the right way: What do you do when you are faced with an adverse situation? There are several options for you, but the best is that you should learn from them. Take your time to consider the lessons you've learned through the negative experience. Even though we should not make the experience the best teacher, most times we tend to repeat the same mistakes others have made. Dissecting what led to the horrible experience from the surface to the core is very important. However, you should avoid moping about the issue over and over in your head because it may cause more regrets than learning. Think about it once or twice and let it go! The bitter truth about this point is that we are not perfect. We keep making mistakes and that is not a crime, but repeating the same mistake is what should be considered as a crime to self-discovery and common sense.

Now that you know exactly what it is you desire in your life, take the time to evaluate your own ability to realize your dreams. How likely are you to get the things/events that you desire in your life? ***Below, list each of your desires in the order that you believe you are capable of achieving them. Start with the ones that you feel confident about and capable of bringing into your life, and move down the list. The desires that you feel confident about will lead the way and pave the road for the rest of them.***

MY CREATION POWER

1.______________________________________

2.______________________________________

3.______________________________________

4.______________________________________

5.______________________________________

6.______________________________________

7.______________________________________

CHAPTER 3

Releasing your full potential

"Often, it's not about becoming a new person but becoming the person, you were meant to be, and already are, but don't know how to be" -Heath L. Buckmaster

I would like to share with you what one of my mentor, my role model, Myles Munroe had to say concerning this topic. The following you are going to read now is an article which appeared in the October 1991 issue of Charisma magazine.

"The wealthiest spot on this planet is not the oil fields of Saudi Arabia or the gold mines of South Africa. The richest deposits on our planet lie not many blocks from your house in your local cemetery. Buried beneath the soil of those sacred grounds are songs that were never sung, books that never were written, paintings that never filled a canvas, and ideas that never became a reality? Tragically, our graveyards are filled with potential that never was fulfilled.

As I walk the streets of our cities, my heart grieves over the wasted, broken, disoriented lives I encounter. During their youth, they had dreams, desires, plans and aspirations; but today, they are lost in a maze of substance abuse, alcoholism, and primarily purposelessness.

Only a small percentage of the 5 billion people on this planet will achieve a significant portion of their true potential. Their potential remains untapped because they do not understand the nature of the *potential principle: potential is not what you have done, but what you can do. Not what is, but what could be.*

What is potential? *Dormant ability, Untapped strength, Unused success, Hidden talents, Capped capability*

Define potential according to your own understanding

____

____

____

____

____

____

There's a wealth of potential within you. But you must decide if you will deprive the world or bless it with the valuable, potent, untapped resources locked away within you. Most men and women never realize their full potential because they don't understand the keys to a fulfilled and effective life.

You have a multitude of hidden talents that you may not use as much as you could. Remember what you are good at to reclaim your superpowers. They will help you overcome your limiting beliefs.

Below, list all your amazing abilities that have taken you this far. Think of all the challenging situations that you have

experienced and how you have handled them. Also, think about what people appreciate about you. If you don't know, ask the people who know you the best.

MY STRONGEST POINT

____

____

____

____

____

____

Every manufacturer establishes the specifications, environment, conditions and operational standards for attaining the maximum performance level of his or her product. God, our creator, and manufacturer, has also established a plan for the maximum performance and release of your potential. Violation of these requirements will result in the malfunction, distortion, misuse and abuse of your precious potential.

After careful study of the Bible - the Manufacturer's Handbook - I have identified 10 major keys to releasing your full potential:

You must know (be related to) your source. It is essential that you understand the nature, composition, and consistency of your source, for this is the key to understanding the potency of your potential. If you had a wooden table in your house, for example, you would be aware that the table is made of wood from a tree. The strength, durability, and nature of the table can only be as strong and durable as the tree. If the tree is weak, the table will be the same. Therefore, the potential of the table is determined by the potential of the source from which it came. The same goes for you. To understand how much potential you possess, the qualities and nature of our source have to be capable of manifesting these qualities. We also possess an eternal spirit just like our source. We live forever not because He allows us to, but because it is our nature. . .

You must understand how much product was designed to function. Every manufacturer designs, develop and produces his or her product to function in a particular manner. Automobile manufacturers, for instance, design their products to function with gasoline, spark plugs, batteries, pistons, oil, water and so forth. No matter what you do, if you do not supply the elements required for the operational function of the product, it will not perform and maximize its potential. God designs human beings to function as He does. You and I were created to function by faith and love. These are the fuels on which we run... Our potential cannot be released without faith and love. Fear and hatred short-circuit our potential.

You must know your purpose. Every product exists for a particular purpose. That reason is the original intent of its existence, the purpose of which the manufacturer made it. Knowing the manufacturer's intent is essential because the purpose for which something was made determines its design, nature, and potential.

God created you and gave you a life for a purpose. Whatever that purpose is, you possess the potential to fulfill it. No matter how big the dream God gave you, your potential is equal to the assignment. Purpose gives birth to responsibility, and responsibility makes demands on potential.

You must understand your resources. All manufacturers provide access to the necessary resources for the proper maintenance, sustenance, and operation of their products. Resources and provisions are to help sustain the product while its potential is being maximized. God, in His great wisdom, provided human beings with great material and physical resources to support and maintain us as we proceed in realizing, developing and maximizing our potential. We are never to worship the resources, nor are we to be controlled by them. Idolatry and substance abuse are violations of the Manufacturer's specifications and will lead to the destruction of potential.

You must have the right environment. The environment consists of the conditions that have a direct or indirect effect on the performance, function, and development of a thing. Every manufacturer specifies the proper conditions under which he or she guarantees the maximum performance of the product. In the manual, the manufacturer will caution against violation of that specified environment for maximum performance. The right environment is the ideal conditions needed to maximize the true potential. . . God designed humans to function in the garden of His presence, in a relationship with Him, free from sin and in daily communion with His Spirit. Human potential needs this positive environment of fellowship, relationship, love and challenge to be maximized. You can never be all you could be in any other environment. He sent the Holy Spirit to restore our internal environment, the key to realizing your true potential is the restoration of God's original environment.

You must work out your potential. Potential is dormant ability, but ability is useless until it is given responsibility. When God created Adam, He planted in him the potential to subdue, rule over and care for the earth and everything in it. This purpose predetermined his potential. Adam had inside of him all the potential necessary to fulfill the assignment, but he was not aware of his potential, even as you may not be aware of what you can do. Work is a major key to releasing your potential. Claiming a promise does not make it happen. You must apply the principle of work. The land was promised to the children of Israel, but they had to walk it out to possess it. Good ideas do not bring success. Good hard work does. To release your true potential, you must be willing to work.

You must cultivate your potential. Potential is like a seed. It is a hidden ability that needs to be cultivated. You must feed your potential the fertilizer of positive company, give it the environment of encouragement, drench it with the water of God's Word and bathe it in the sunshine of personal prayer. Read materials that stimulate your faith and nourish your dream.

You must guard your potential. It's tragic when a tree dies in a seed, or a person dies in childhood. It's sad when what could have been turns out to be what should have been. With all the wealth of your potential, you must be careful to guard and protect it. The Bible calls your potential a treasure in an earthen vessel. You must guard your visions and dreams against sin, discouragement, procrastination, failures, opinions, distractions, traditions and compromise. Satan is after your potential. Be on guard.

You must share your potential. God created the heavens and the earth to operate on this principle: potential can only be fulfilled when it is shared. Nature abounds with this truth. The sun does not exist for itself. Plants release oxygen for us, and we provide carbon dioxide for the plants. The bee receives nectar as it pollinates the flowers. No potential exists for itself. This is also true to human potential. The true measure of fulfilled potential is not what is accomplished, but who receives benefit from the accomplishment. Your deposit was given to enrich and inspire the lives of others. Remember, the great law is love.

You must know and understand the laws of limitation. Freedom and power are two of the most important elements in our lives. Potential is the essence of both. Potential is power. But freedom needs a law to be enjoyed, and power needs responsibility to be effective. One without the other produces self-destruction. Every manufacturer establishes laws of limitations. These laws are not given to restrict, but to protect, not to hinder, but to assist and guarantee the maximum performance of potential. God has set laws and standards to protect our potential and to secure our success. Violating these laws limits the release of your potential. Obedience ensures protection and maximization. Commit yourself to obeying the manufacturer. Then watch your life unfold as you discover the hidden ability that was always within you."

Your beliefs are crucial in creating the life you want to live. Your life is a direct projection of your belief system. When you expose the beliefs that are keeping you from realizing your desires you understand what you need to let go of. ***Below, list the limiting beliefs that keep you from realizing your desires. Also, try to identify why you have created these beliefs in the first place? Do they stem from bad experiences, family programming or have you just been taught by others to think in a certain way?***

MY LIMITING BELIEF

____

____

____

____

____

We understand that everything in life was created with potential and possesses the potential principle. We also defined potential as dormant ability, untapped strength, unused success, hidden talents, capped capability. We have explored 10 ways to releasing your potential by Myles Munroe. But I want to offer some tips which can also help you in realizing your maximum potential. These are:

Making a conscious choice to pursue your personal growth. Making a decision like these changes you and makes you move forward. This choice to pursue your personal growth is what should push you to read books like these, blogs, listen to audio books and attend seminars. You should get materials and mentors to help you.

Set a goal to work toward. Goals are powerful instruments which can change the course of your life. When you don't have a concrete goal, you begin to feel aimless. But when you narrow your mind to what you can achieve, you start to release your potential to its maximum level. Delaying an action when it comes to realizing your goals can also be harmful to the journey of your self-discovery.

Take little steps. Now, you have something to aim for your goals. What is next is to take action. When you begin to take action, it shows that you are building evidence to show that your mind can do more than you imagine. A good way to begin with little steps is by having role models, those who have already done what you like and are successful. Learn from them. You can check their blogs, read their books, attend their training/coaching programs. Building your mind is pivotal to releasing your full potential. Having a mentor too can help accelerate your growing process.

Make sure you have a success list. An achievement list is the compilation of all your accomplishments or achievements. We all love to feel fulfilled and satisfied with ourselves. A success list gives us a lot of confidence that we can do more. Make sure you input all your achievements no matter how big or small they are. It would happen that you may start to lose confidence in yourself, and that is when the success list comes in handy. Take a good look at it and think positive things to yourself. This can help you face your fears and achieve what you think is impossible.

Think about everything you have successfully completed, list them out and rethink over it so you can recall how you made it work

1.________________________________

2.________________________________

3.________________________________

4.________________________________

5.________________________________

Set your own benchmark. No accomplishment is too small. Be proud of your accomplishment, set your own benchmark and be happy with yourself. Comparing yourself to other people could make your achievement seem insignificant; avoid it. If you feel that you have just surmounted Mount Kilimanjaro, well some just reached the peak of Everest. It's an endless cycle. Be happy with your progress. It is normal some would improve faster than others, so don't compare yourself with others. Life is not a sprint, it's a marathon, and there is enough opportunity for everyone. The sky is sufficient for all birds to fly without disturbing each other. Your focus should be on what you can do to improve yourself, to add more value to yourself and others. Make sure you continue to grow, set your goals, move forward, take one step at a time and continue to impress yourself.

I would like to wrap up this chapter using the words of Oliver Wendell Holmes. *"What lies behind us and what lies before us are tiny matters, compared to what lies within us."*

You have more than what it takes to be great! Know your purpose and unlock your potential.

Your motivation is what will bring you closer to creating the life you want to live. By understanding why you want the things/events that you have listed in previous steps you will understand their importance. Your motivation becomes the fuel that powers your engine. The most powerful motivators are connected to your soul's desire rather than your ego.

Explain what motivates you to realize your GOALS AND DESIRES? How will you feel once you have achieved your desires? How will your life change?

MY MOTIVATION

1.____

2.____

3.____

4.____

5.____

6.____

7.____

8.____

9.____

10.____

CHAPTER 4

Getting Over It

"Trust yourself. You know more than you think you do."-Benjamin Spock

This chapter would expose you to ways to feel better about yourself. Simply put, self-esteem. The ideal thing is not only to discover your potential, but to understand it and realize it to full potential. You would also need to be happy with the real you, the true you. That is where "getting over it" comes in. Overcoming trauma and feeling good about yourself is quite easier than you may think. The problem is that we think too much, we allow our present to overwhelm us, we don't dream of a bright future, or even if we dream about that bright future, the present is so strong to the extent that we can't see the bright side of things.

Below, draw your life vision; the new reality that you are creating. Keep your finished drawing in a place where you can view it every single day. It will remind you of your

desires and the overall vision that you have set for your life.

MY VISION

With more than enough negativity or negative reinforcement from ourselves first and others, we begin to train ourselves to see only our mistakes, our flaws, our failures. I mentioned being innocent in a particular chapter; now I want you to cast your mind back to when you were little, precisely 3 years or 4. Remember that you landed on this Earth with more than enough exuberance to last us for life. All we needed was just a little food, little comfort, and a clean bottom. Well, all that has changed drastically because constantly we begin to feel 'less' of ourselves. If our training to feel bad about ourselves continues, feeling good becomes far from us. So, what can we do? Can we unlearn the old beliefs which have placed us in this mess? Can we see our own beauty and worthiness? Yes, Yes and Yes.

Walt Whitman says "I celebrate myself and sing myself."

ACTIONS POINTS

- ✓ We need to celebrate ourselves making use of the following ways right now.
- ✓ **Look in the mirror:** See your best features, your curves, your eyes, your hair, and not your physical flaws, be grateful for it.
- ✓ **Call your mother:** She loves us most than we can imagine for most of us, give her a call. Talk to your family members, enjoy their presence.
- ✓ **List your achievements:** we have mentioned that earlier. It makes you feel good about yourself.
- ✓ **Do a 5-minute exercise:** Exercise should not be intimidating. Anywhere you find yourself in the gym or anywhere else. Boost your energy.
- ✓ **Write a love note:** This may sound weird to you but knowing how important you are to someone or how someone is important to you, makes you feel really good. Share your love; it makes you feel lovable.

- ✓ **Relive your best memory: This** can be done physically or mentally. You can visit that place you couldn't stop visiting each day when you were a child or a teenager. Take your time to reminisce on your best moment in life

- ✓ **Don't compare yourself.** You should not compare yourself to the 1% of the population or even less. Focus on yourself.

- ✓ **Smile:** This is paramount. Scientist has been able to discover that smile affects your health and increases the number of years you would spend on earth. Although these sounds bizarre but a warm smile could do more magic than you think.

Make a list of your good qualities

____

____

____

____

The most important thing of feeling good about yourself is that you should give yourself pure pleasure every day. This is key to living a healthy life and realizing your greatest potential and purpose

Your vision will guide you in the process of creating a new reality. By verbalizing your vision, you will amplify your creation powers. Words are powerful and everything that you ask for from a heart-centered place that is free from fear and doubt will happen.

Below, put your life vision into words by creating a few affirmations that describe the new reality that you are creating. Keep these affirmations in a place where you can read them out loud every single day.

MY AFFIRMATIONS

____

____

____

____